The Puffin Patrol

The Puffin Patrol

written and illustrated by
DAWN BAKER

Pennywell Books
St. John's

Library and Archives Canada Cataloguing in Publication

Baker, Dawn, 1962-, author illustrator
The Puffin Patrol / written and illustrated by Dawn Baker.

Issued in print and electronic formats.
ISBN 978-1-77117-605-7 (paperback).--ISBN 978-1-77117-606-4 (pdf)

A CIP catalogue record for this book is available from Library and Archives Canada

---

PRINTED IN CANADA

MIX
Paper from responsible sources
FSC® C016245
FSC www.fsc.org

This paper has been certified to meet the environmental and social standards of the Forest Stewardship Council® (FSC®) and comes from responsibly managed forests, and verified recycled sources.

Pennywell Books is an imprint of Flanker Press Limited.

FLANKER PRESS LTD.
PO BOX 2522, STATION C
ST. JOHN'S, NL A1C 6K1 CANADA

TELEPHONE: (709) 739-4477 TOLL-FREE: 1-866-739-4420 FAX: (709) 739-4420

WWW.FLANKERPRESS.COM

9 8 7 6 5 4 3 2 1

Cover Design: Peter Hanes

Canada
Canada Council for the Arts / Conseil des Arts du Canada
Newfoundland Labrador

We acknowledge the [financial] support of the Government of Canada. *Nous reconnaissons l'appui [financier] du gouvernement du Canada*. We acknowledge the support of the Canada Council for the Arts, which last year invested $153 million to bring the arts to Canadians throughout the country. *Nous remercions le Conseil des arts du Canada de son soutien. L'an dernier, le Conseil a investi 153 millions de dollars pour mettre de l'art dans la vie des Canadiennes et des Canadiens de tout le pays*. We acknowledge the financial support of the Government of Newfoundland and Labrador, Department of Tourism, Culture and Recreation for our publishing activities.

I would like to thank the following:

Suzanne Dooley and everyone with the Newfoundland Chapter of the Canadian Parks and Wilderness Society. http://cpawsnl.org

Molly Bawn Whale & Puffin Tours. https://mollybawn.com

Newfoundsander blogger and photographer. https://newfoundsander.wordpress.com

And last but most certainly not least,
Juergen and Elfie Schau, who started the Puffin Patrol in Witless Bay!

Susan couldn't help but smile. She looked over at her friend Ryan and saw that he was also smiling. It was a cool, damp night in late August and the two should have been warm in their beds. Instead, they were about to go roaming around gloomy streets and gardens with Ryan's older sister, Megan.

Megan had been working with the Puffin Patrol for over two weeks, and this was the first night that the two young friends would get to help.

They would all be going on a mission. A rescue mission! Everyone would be searching for baby puffins that needed their help.

The Puffin Patrol operates every summer in Witless Bay, a small community on the shores of the island of Newfoundland.

After dark, volunteers search roadsides and backyards on the lookout for lost pufflings. When one is spotted, it is gently captured and carefully placed in a plastic crate until it can be safely released the next morning. Sometimes they are released from shore and sometimes from tour boats farther out on the ocean.

Susan and Ryan had learned how the pufflings leave their cozy burrows at night to take their first flights. On clear nights, the pufflings use the stars to guide them safely out to sea.

But when the nights are cloudy and the stars are hidden, these sweet little birds see the lights from the shore and fly the wrong way. Instead of landing on the ocean, the pufflings find themselves stranded throughout towns along the coast. The members of the Puffin Patrol do their best to locate these lost baby puffins and help them find their way to the ocean.

Ryan suddenly waved at Susan and pointed to the edge of a flower bed. There was a puffling huddled behind a plant!

The two friends spoke softly to the small bird while Ryan lifted it up from the ground and placed it in a crate. As the night wore on, the Puffin Patrol found twelve more lost little ones, and each was placed in its own crate for the night.

Before they would be set free, the pufflings would be banded, weighed, measured, and tested for bird flu. This was a task Megan really enjoyed.

By the time Susan got to bed, it was very late. Although she had walked a good while and was very tired, she still couldn't sleep. She was so excited about the next day. The following morning, she and Ryan were going on a tour boat to help release the pufflings out at sea. Susan could hardly wait!

The next morning brought sunshine and warmer temperatures. Still, the two friends brought their jackets with them to wear on the tour boat, because even on warm days it can be cold on the Atlantic Ocean! Once the boat with its precious cargo had motored a long way from shore, it slowed almost to a stop.

Megan slowly opened the crates and very gently gave a puffling to Susan and one to Ryan.

Susan was super careful as she moved to the rail on the boat. She lifted her arms high and, as she had been taught, tossed the baby puffin into the sky! It spread its wings and flew even higher before changing direction and diving into the sea.

Then Susan watched as it bobbed back up and floated on the ocean surface. The rescue mission was a great success! The puffling was back home. Other puffins and pufflings were flying and bobbing on the water and diving. They all seemed to be having a great time!

Now it was Ryan's turn to release a baby puffin. He could not have been happier. It was so much fun!

Later that year, Susan and Ryan returned to Witless Bay with their families for the weekend. The two friends walked along the shore and talked about their busy summer.

All the pufflings would be grown by now and heading even farther out to sea for the winter.

Susan felt a warm glow as she imagined the colourful birds returning to Newfoundland in the spring. Some would be making the journey thanks to her and Ryan and all of the volunteers with the Puffin Patrol.

It was a great feeling! Once again, Susan couldn't keep the smile from her face.

SLOW
DOWN!
BABY
PUFFINS
ON
ROAD
BE AWARE

Did you know?

A group of puffins may be called a circus.

Pufflings are not as colourful as adult puffins and have smaller beaks.

An adult puffin can hold ten fish in its beak at once.

Puffins mate for life.

Each pair of puffins lays just one egg per year.

Puffins can fly nearly ninety kilometres per hour.

Puffins can flap their wings 400 times each minute.

Puffins can dive up to seventy metres.

An adult puffin is shorter (from bill to tail) than the average blue jay but weighs over four times as much!

The Atlantic puffin is the official bird of the province of Newfoundland and Labrador.

The Witless Bay Ecological Reserve has the largest Atlantic puffin colony in North America with over 260,000 mating pairs!

How can you help?

If you live near a nesting site—southeast Newfoundland coast:

Reduce all unnecessary lighting.

Use down-facing lights outside.

Change to coloured bulbs, especially amber, red, or blue.

Install motion-sensor lighting.

Drive very slowly August through September, when pufflings are leaving their burrows.

Wherever you live:

All of the above will help all wild birds.

Keep plastic out of your trash. Remember: always reduce, reuse, recycle!

Learn more about the Puffin Patrol!

Dawn Baker has been a visual artist and children's writer since 1992. A graduate of Memorial University, she has served on the board of directors of The Rooms Corporation of Newfoundland and Labrador since 2006. In 2015, Dawn served as a juror for the Governor General's Literary Awards in Children's Literature – Illustrated Books and toured Ontario as part of TD Canadian Children's Book Week.

Over 80,000 books sold!

Also by Dawn Baker

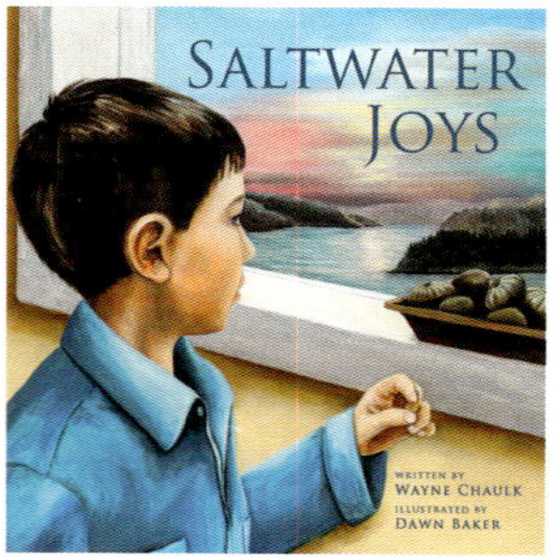

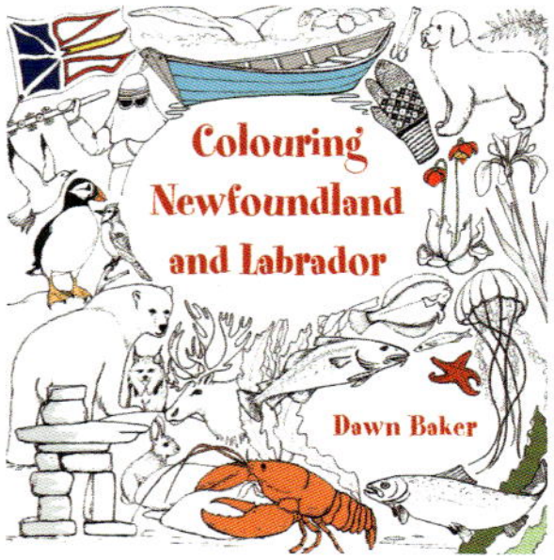